WHAT I LOVE ABOUT YOU
♥

WHAT I LOVE ABOUT YOU

♥

A BOOK TO
PERSONALISE
FOR SOMEONE
YOU LOVE

A STUDIO PRESS BOOK

First published in the UK in 2018 by Studio Press,
an imprint of Bonnier Books UK,
The Plaza, 535 King's Road, London SW10 0SZ
Owned by Bonnier Books
Sveavägen 56, Stockholm, Sweden

www.studiopressbooks.co.uk
www.bonnierpublishing.co.uk

7 9 10 8

ISBN 978-1-78741-372-6

Originally published in German by riva Verlag, an imprint of
Münchner Verlagsgruppe GmbH in 2015

A CIP catalogue for this book is available from the British Library
Printed and bound in Lithuania

"Silence is golden."

As the saying implies, all too often words simply fail us – especially when we are searching for the right ones! This happens even though there are so many things we want to tell our other half: how much we admire them, how much they delight and surprise us, and how much we love them. Despite all this, it is sometimes hard to pause for a moment, take our partner's hand and express just how we feel. Most of the time their hand is busy doing the washing-up, typing away or midway through cooking dinner – it is just never the right time. And even when the most perfect moment arises – like watching the sunset from a bench in the garden – then seldom do we manage more than an awkward, 'I love you'.

Now is the time for that to change! Everyone who is in love has their own story, a shared love story, which deserves to be written down. And everyone has hundreds of compliments for their other half that they never find the words to say. Now you can fill these pages and create the greatest love story of all time. There is nothing more beautiful than love – let us celebrate it!

PS. If you think it is high time that you got your own love story, then simply give this book (and a pen!) to your other half.

Have fun!

—————————O—————————

This book was filled out by

_____

for

_____

as a sign of our love.

Together since: _____

Started this diary on:_____

—————————O—————————

My heart is yours.

The first time I saw you I thought:

....

....

After our first meeting, the thing that surprised me most about you was:

....

....

....

This song always reminds me of our first meeting:

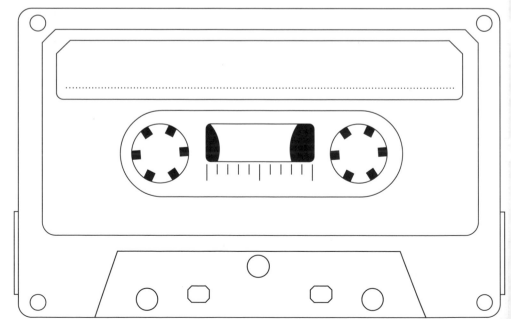

My favourite part of you is:

You are different from everyone else because:

....

....

....

The first person I told about you was:

....

This is what I told them:

....

....

....

This is what I looked like on the inside when we met:

I was really jealous when:

....

....

....

....

....

....

Our first photo together:

I would love to travel with you to:

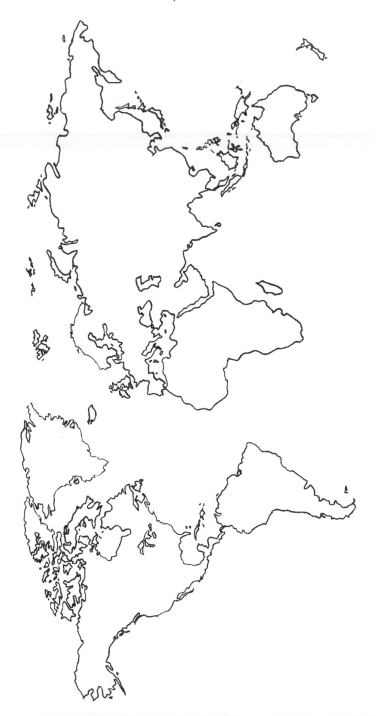

On a scale of 0-10, I find you: (0 = not at all, 10 = extremely)

Good-looking [   ]   Honest [   ]

Funny [   ]   Charming [   ]

Loyal [   ]   Sexy [   ]

The best joke you have ever told is:

....

....

....

"My heart is ever at your service."
William Shakespeare

This is what I really like to do with you:

On the weekend: ....

On holiday: ....

On a normal weekday: ....

On a sunny Sunday: ....

On a rainy Sunday: ....

At night: ....

I hid this characteristic from you the longest:

....

....

....

....

When we are apart, I miss you after:

Years [　　　]   Minutes [　　　]

Months [　　　]   Seconds [　　　]

Days [　　　]   As soon as we part [　　　]

Hours [　　　]

When we met I tried my best to be:

....

I have never told you that:

....

....

....

Here is my drawing of your celebrity lookalike:

It is supposed to be:

....

When I dream about you, I dream about:

....

....

....

Exactly this amount of my
heart belongs to you:

The first time I wanted to sleep with you was when:

....

....

....

Our first holiday was in: ....

The thing I remember most from that holiday is:

....

....

I like it when we wake up in the morning and:

....

....

The moment I fell in love with you was when:

....

Everyone realised I was in love when:

....

The first time I realised that you liked me was when you:

....

At the beginning of our relationship, these friends already thought we made a nice couple:

....

....

I could eat you up when you:

....

I think the secret to our relationship is:

....

The most beautiful thing you have ever said to me is:

....

....

....

I would give you this much
of my pizza:

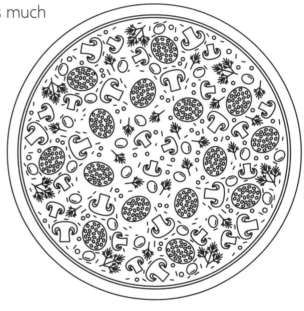

If I could relive one day of our relationship again it

would be: ....

....

....

....

....

If you were an animal, you would be a:

....

A difficult time for us was when:

....

....

You helped me the most when:

....

....

───────○───────

"But we loved with a love that was more than love."
Edgar Allan Poe

───────○───────

If I could give you anything, it would be:

....

....

I would pay this much ransom money to get you back:

£..

With you by my side, my glass is never empty. Instead, it is approximately this full:

And it contains:

....

For me, you are like:

This time of year: ....

This ice-cream flavour: ....

This film: ....

This weekday: ....

This book: ....

This drink: ....

This colour: ....

This plant: ....

I was scared/worried for you when:

....

....

I think you would be incredibly successful in this career:

....

I think that because: ....

....

....

I felt incredibly in love with you in this moment:

....

....

....

....

I will never forget this celebration with you:

....

Because you: ....

....

....

My favourite outfit of yours is:

I think highly of you for:

....

....

....

When I close my eyes and think of you, I see:

....

....

I love this quirk of yours:

....

....

You are always happy when I cook this recipe:

....

....

....

....

....

....

....

....

....

....

....

If you were born again, you would be:

....

And I would be: ....

In your past life you were probably:

....

If we were a couple from a film, we would be:

☐ Laurel and Hardy   ☐ Baby and Johnny

☐ Sandy and Danny   ☐ Beauty and the Beast

☐ Cinderella and Prince Charming   ☐ Leia and Hans

☐ Elizabeth and Darcy   ☐ ....

If I imagine you as a child, I picture you as:

....

———————○———————

"Love is composed of a single soul inhabiting two bodies."
Aristotle

———————○———————

I remember this night of passion most fondly:

....

....

....

I know that you want to be alone with me when you:

....

....

When I picture us in 20 years' time, it looks something like this:

A special anniversary for us is:

....

You can do ....
.... a lot better than me.

Without you, I would only be this tall:

```
10
9
8
7
6
5
4
3
2
1
0
```

My favourite story about you is:

....

....

....

....

....

....

I would love to have these characteristics of yours:

....

....

....

When I'm alone without you, I: ....

....

If I could only say one sentence to you in this lifetime, then
I would say: ....

....

I would have never expected you to know so much about:

....

Since we met, you have become better at:

....

....

If I were to lead a totally different life with you, we would:

....

....

If you liked it, I would call you this pet name:

....

My favourite photo of you:

And my favourite photo of us:

> *"There is only one happiness in this life, to love and be loved."*
> *George Sand*

If I got a tattoo to symbolise our love, then it would look like this:

I am so sorry that I:

....

....

....

....

It is always fun when we:

....

....

....

A turn of phrase that you always use and I like to hear is:

....

....

....

I hope you never ask me to do this, but for you I would:

....

....

....

It turns me on to imagine you like this:

....

....

I have never asked you this but have always wanted to

know: ....

....

A wonderful characteristic of yours that not many people

notice is: ....

....

....

If you were a country, you would be:

....

One of my happiest memories was when you:

....

....

....

If you were a car, you would be a:

....

You would be this emoji:

One day when we are old we will live in ....

and we will spend all our time ....

.... and ....

You look so good when you:

....

....

If I had met you sooner:

....

....

....

I would still love you even if you looked like this:

You are:

As beautiful as: ....

As wild as: ....

As brave as: ....

As strong as: ....

And as sweet as: ....

"Ladies and gentlemen, we are here today to thank a very

special person: .... We are so grateful that:

....

....

....

....

....

....

....

....

Thank you."

The gemstone that suits you best is:

....

I swear on my life that I will:

....

And I will never: ....

You would make a great character in this TV series:

....

In which you would play:...

The last time we laughed so hard we cried was when:

....

....

....

If you were a drug you would be: ....

If money were no object, then we would:

....

....

You know this better than anyone else on Earth:

....

Our coat of arms would look like this:

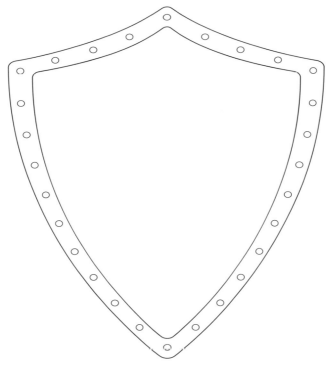

When you look in the mirror, I hope you see that:

....

....

....

Without you, I would never have had the courage to:

....

....

....

I was so impressed when you: ....

....

....

....

Thank you for loving me even though I:

....

....

....

I admire you for: ....

....

....

One day we should definitely do this:

....

....

....

If I had to give you a new first name, I would call you:

....

I know you are a good person when you:

....

....

....

....

I love it when you make this face:

You make this face when: ....

Do you remember that time we got really drunk together?
It was when: ....

....

....

....

I think that your soul looks like this:

If you were a fairy-tale character you would be:

....

Because: ....

....

....

Our love is:

☐ So-so   ☐ Fine thanks

☐ Alright   ☐ The best thing that ever happened to me

The first place we saw each other was:

....

....

You looked like: ....

....

When I saw you I really liked:

....

....

If I imagine the perfect day, then it would be:

....

....

....

....

....

An experience I want to share with you is:

....

....

....

Thank you for making this possible:

....

....

....

Sometimes I worry that you:

....

....

....

When we get old and look back on our life together,
I hope you will say:

....

....

Other people compliment you for:

....

....

....

....

....

You smell as good as: ....

Since you came into my life, it has been:

☐ Funnier   ☐ More chaotic

☐ Easier   ☐ Calmer

☐ Sweeter   ☐ More romantic

☐ More colourful   ☐ Sillier

☐ Sexier   ☐ _____

You are so funny when you: ....

....

....

No one is as good at this as you: ....

You are always surprising me. The last time was when:

....

....

I will never forget the moment when: ....

....

....

When you enter the room:

....

If you were my best friend's other half, then I would:

....

....

....

When I am sad, you comfort me by:..

....

I was so happy you were with me when:

....

....

....

Do you remember this romantic dinner?

....

....

....

If an artist painted you, then they would definitely
emphasise your: ....

....

I was especially proud of you when:

....

....

....

My favourite text message from you was:

....

....

....

....

....

If you were a food, you would be: ....

The most beautiful place we have visited together was:

....

....

....

....

....

I missed you the most when:

....

....

....

....

You really helped these people when they needed you:

....

....

I would immediately appoint you to this political position:

....

The best gift you have ever given me was:

....

You made me so happy when you:

....

The best advice you have ever given me was:

....

An important step in our relationship was when:

....

Thank you for being so friendly to:

....

If the world was going to end tomorrow and we only had one more day, then I would like to spend it like this:

....

....

....

....

I would even go to a .... concert for you.

I always think of you when I hear these words:

....

These people would pay the following compliments to you:

Your mother:..

Your father:...

Your friends:...

Your kids:...

Your sister:...

Your brother:...

Your boss:...

Your colleagues:..

Your old teacher:...

With your family, you handle..

....so well.

I love this secret that we both keep:

I think ....

....

.... looks really good on you.

This criticism you made of me really helped me:

....

....Thank you.

Sometimes I worry that you will leave me one day because
of: ....

I would love to start this hobby with you: ....

....

I would love to experience this with you:

....

....

....

I think the best thing I have done in my life was:

....

....

....

My favourite meal that you make is: ....

....

If I were invisible for a day, then I would most like to watch
you: ....

I love you even if I sometimes laugh at you, like when you:

....

In our dream house there would definitely be a:

....

I would kick .... out of my bed for you.

If you were going to pose for a naked photo, then I'd picture you:

☐ Lying on a bear rug in front of the fireplace

☐ Under a waterfall

☐ Wrapped in silk sheets

☐ In uniform

☐ Swinging a whip

☐ On a galloping horse

You are so relaxed when it comes to:..

I admire this about you:

This characteristic: ....

This memory: ....

This family member: ....

This talent:..

This friend:...

And:...

This landscape captures you the best:

☐	Forest	☐	Rainforest
☐	Sea	☐	Plains
☐	Mountains	☐	Glacier
☐	Desert	☐	_____

─────────○─────────

"There is always some madness in love."
Friedrich Nietzsche

─────────○─────────

If I saw you for the first time today, I would think:

....

....

For you, I would like to be more:

....

....

Since we have been together, I have been:

....

....

Because I really love you, I will always give you:

....

I am so happy that you:

Never: ....

Always: ....

Sometimes: ....

Each letter of your first name stands for a word that describes you (for example, 'S' for 'strong'):

.... stands for ....

.... stands for ....

.... stands for ....

.... stands for ....

.... stands for ....

.... stands for ....

.... stands for ....

.... stands for ....

.... stands for ....

.... stands for ....

.... stands for ....

It is great that we both enjoy doing these things:

....

....

....

Neither of us enjoys doing these things:

....

....

....

I like the way you say: ....

I have tried so many new things because of you, such as:

This meal: ....

This drink: ....

This book: ....

This film: ....

This place: ....

I have also learned how to be .... because of you.

This is what I have learned about myself because of you:

....

Because of you, I have learned to see some things differently. For example, I have changed my opinion about:

This person: ....

This career path: ....

This relationship: ....

This pastime: ....

And: ....

If I could go back in time to change one thing in our relationship, it would be:

....

I would give anything to see you:

☐ Happier ☐ Relaxed ☐ Successful

☐ Laughing ☐ Turned on ☐ ....

The colour I like best on you is: ....

I find you totally irresistible when you sleep like this:

The experience that bonded us the most was:

....

....

....

....

....

....

....

....

If you were going to get a tattoo and I could choose where to put it, I would choose:

....

And it would be a picture of: ....

You are welcome to:

☐ My money

☐ My love

☐ My smartphone

☐ A kidney

☐ All my loyalty points

☐ My social media passwords

☐ Custody of the dog

☐ ....

In the future, I really want to experience this important moment with you: ....

....

....

I remember this special phone call:

....

....

....

The colour of your eyes reminds me of:

....

....

I think your IQ is about: ....

The first film we saw together was:

I am so happy you stay level-headed when I:

....

Over time, our relationship has become:

....

My favourite small tradition of ours is:

....

....

The thing you do that impresses me the most is:

....

....

....

I like it when you tell this story:

....

....

....

....

With you as my role model, I am now more.............................

.... than I was before we met.

I wish I had listened to you when you said:

....

....

Before we kick the bucket, we should definitely:

....

....

I think we get on as well as:

....

....

....

———○———

"The happiness of life is made up of minute fractions."
Samuel Taylor Coleridge

———○———

I like doing this for you:

....

....

Without you I would never have experienced:

....

....

....

I really appreciate that you stopped doing this for me:

....

One of the first things you said to me was:

....

....

You are:

☐ The seasoning in my soup   ☐ The chilli in my eyes

☐ The pepper on my steak

I love you from here to here:

I want to improve this in the future:

....

....

This is what gets me hot under the collar:

☐ A roaring fire ☐ You, naked.

☐ A cup of tea ☐ ....

I like your style when you:

....

....

The best relationship advice I ever received about us was

from: ....

And they said: ....

....

One day, please can you teach me how to:

....

....

If there is one thing I want, it is:

☐ To make you happy ☐ Immortality

☐ Superpowers ☐ To be rich and famous

I am so happy that our relationship is nothing like that of:

....

....

Sometimes I just want to give you a hug, but I can't because we are:

☐ Standing in the frozen section at the supermarket   ☐ Stuck in a traffic jam

☐ In the doctor's waiting room   ☐ ....

Thank goodness we set the record straight in our relationship about: ....

....

We always have this at home: ....

We never have this at home: ....

Our shared weaknesses are:

....

....

I think your star sign should actually be:

I think that because: ....
....

I wish I had been there to see this moment in your life:

....

....

....

....

If I were your fairy godmother (don't laugh at me for having wings and a wand), then I would grant you these three wishes:

1. ....

2. ....

3. ....

The biggest mistake we ever made was:

....

....

....

From it we learned that:

....

....

....

When time travel finally becomes possible, I want to travel to this moment in time with you:

....

So that we could: ....

....

....

If I could only describe our love with one word, then I would choose: ....

Because: ....

....

And if I could only describe you with one word, then I would choose: ....

Because: ....

....

I have kept a souvenir from when we: ....

....

....

As well as my other half, you are also my: ....

....

....

I hope that I can be more than just your partner and that

I am also: ....

....

....

Our children, their birthdays and their names:

.................................., ..., ...

.................................., ..., ...

.................................., ..., ...

Or we have no children, but if we did they would be called:

Boy: ....

Girl: ....

What we are best at: ....

....

....

The earth needs rain, the sun needs light, the sky needs stars and I need:

| | Low-fat cheese, urgently

| | To be left in peace

| | You!

This person admires you: ....

They admire you because: ....

....

....

I found it very romantic when you:

....

....

....

....

....

Our first pet is/was/will be:

We had such a good time when we:

....

....

....

....

A photo of us that always makes me laugh:

A happy moment for us was when: ....

....

....

....

Our favourite bar is:

....

And we drink:

....

If I were writing your biography, I would call it:

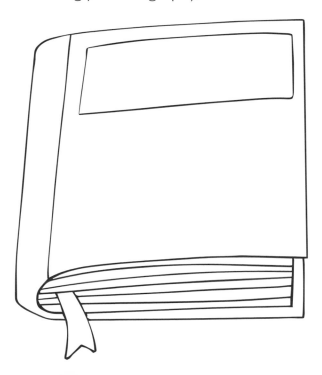

The loveliest compliment you have ever given me was:

....

....

....

There was a time when I was really down, but you were there for me and loved me in spite of it all. That was when:

....

....

....

Thank you.

When you are with your friends, I think it is great that you:

....

....

....

When you are with your family, I think it is great that you:

....

....

....

This is how I look when I think of you:

I think it is great how involved you are with:

....

My wish for us this year is:

....

....

....

....

....

"'Tis better to have loved and lost
Than never to have loved at all."
Alfred Lord Tennyson

I know that you would like me to do this less: ....

....

And to do this more: ....

I promise I will make an effort.

I think you have great taste in:

....

Our first kiss was: ....

We were: ....

And then: ....

....

When we go out I feel: ....

....

If I were making a playlist for you, I would put these songs on it:

....

....

....

....

....

....

....

The first time I did this was with you:

....

Our dream house looks like this:

And it would be in this landscape:

I put up with this without a word of complaint because I love you so much:

- [ ] Your embarrassing slippers
- [ ] Your sense of direction
- [ ] Your snoring
- [ ] Your love of films about ....
- [ ] Your collection of ....
- [ ] ....
- [ ] ....

This person has to come to our wedding (or already has):

....

I will always remember the face you made when:

....

....

You looked very: ....

I know that you were/are jealous of: ....

.... That is unnecessary, my love.

I will try to draw you in all your beauty (keep a straight face!):

The best decision we ever made was:

....

....

....

If you were a time of day, you would be:

I have always remembered this day out:

....

....

....

....

....

On our life journey together we:

☐ Speed off to Vegas in a sports car

☐ Walk off into the sunset

☐ Cycle off together as a perfect team to happiness

☐ Take the first exit and head to the nearest pub

These values are important to us both:

....

....

....

....

I think it is amazing that you have achieved this:

....

....

....

You really helped me with this:

....

....

....

....

Thank you.

The thought I had before our first night together was:

....

....

I would make this road sign for you and put it outside your front door:

I think I am the perfect match for you because:

....

....

I think you are the perfect match for me because:

....

....

When God (or any other power above) created you, they were especially heavy-handed with:

....

---○---

"Be happy for this moment. This moment is your life."
Omar Khayyam

---○---

If, one day, I am no longer around, then I hope you can:

....

....

....

....

....

....

....

When I introduced you to my parents, I felt:

....

....

....

....

....

....

....

I would describe your sense of humour as:

....

....

I would share this with you, even if it cost me the world:

....

When I am feeling low, you always cheer me up by:

....

....

....

When you are feeling low, I can cheer you up by:

....

....

....

I would like to make love to you in these places:

| | Car | | Train | | Swimming pool |

| | Plane | | Forest | | _____ |

I have given this part of your body
a name:

And the name is: ....

(Only joking, I haven't really!)

If we were making a time capsule for us to find in our old
age and remember our relationship by, I would put the
following in it:

....

....

....

....

I know I should say this more often, but I really appreciate that you: ....

....

....

Thank you.

This is how quickly an hour with you passes:

[   ] minutes

This is how slowly an hour without you passes:

[   ] minutes

You are so nice because: ....

....

You are so young because: ....

....

You have the most beautiful ....

.... that I have ever seen.

I find it attractive when you
wear your hair like this:

This was a real adventure that we had together:

....

....

....

....

It was especially good because you:

....

....

On the sign above our bed I would write:

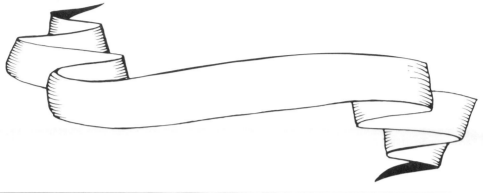

In your messages to me I especially like:

....

....

....

I normally find this awful, but with you by my side it does
not bother me: ....

....

....

If you were a sport, you would be: ....

I think we have given the term ....

.... a new meaning.

I talk to others about you as if you were:

....

I know it is just part of our everyday routine, but I love it when we spend the evenings:

....

....

....

If you mixed up our first names we would become:

....

If there was a website for our love story, it would probably be called: **www.**..**. com**

When you are really enthusiastic about something, it is cute the way you: ....

....

When we met I thought you were .... years old but you were actually.......................years old.

This has improved over the course of our love:

....

....

....

At the very beginning I thought you were: ....

....

.... But that was far from the truth!

You once told me I reminded you of:........................

....

....I liked that!

Now that you have read all of this, I hope that you will come to me and:

....

....

....

....